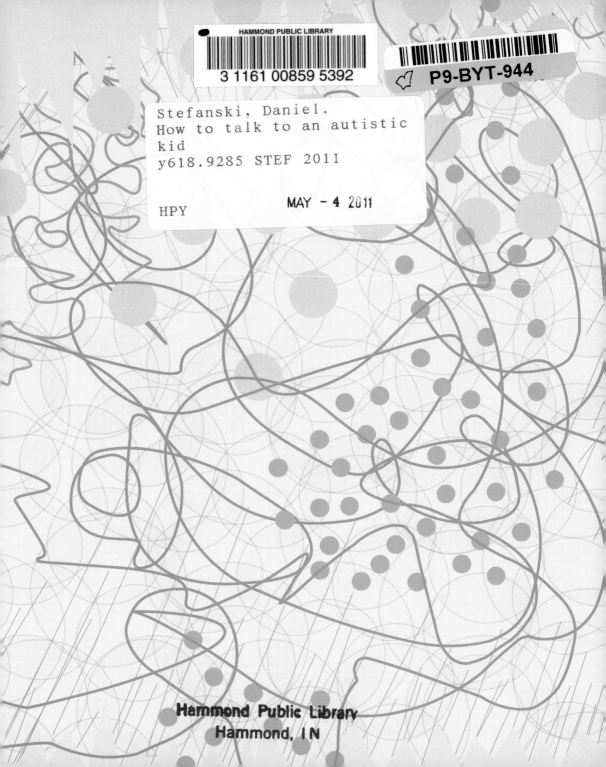

How to Talk to an Autistic Kid

by Daniel Stefanski
(an autistic kid)

free spirit
PUBLISHING®

Library of Congress Cataloging-in-Publication Data
Stefanski, Daniel.
  How to talk to an autistic kid / by Daniel Stefanski ; illustrated by Hazel Mitchell.
    p. cm.
  ISBN 978-1-57542-365-4
  1. Autistic youth. 2. Interpersonal relations. I. Title.
  RJ506.A9S735 2011
  618.92'85882—dc22

                                                    2010043615

eBook ISBN: 978-1-57542-739-3

Edited by Eric Braun
Cover and interior design by Michelle Lee
Illustrations by Hazel Mitchell

Reading Level Grades 3–4; Interest Level Ages 8 to Adult;
Fountas & Pinnell Guided Reading Level P

10 9 8 7 6 5 4 3 2 1
Printed in the United States of America
S13970111

Free Spirit Publishing Inc.
217 Fifth Avenue North, Suite 200
Minneapolis, MN 55401-1299
(612) 338-2068
help4kids@freespirit.com
www.freespirit.com

Dedication

To all kids with autism
and the people who love them.

Acknowledgments

Thank you Dad,
Lee, Matthew, and
Mom, the best mom.

About me and about this book

Hi, I'm Daniel Stefanski, and I'm 14 years old. I have autism. What's that, you ask? Autism is a disorder that affects how my brain works. (Yes, it does work!) My dad, who is an electrical engineer and knows a lot about wires and circuits, told me having autism means that my brain is wired differently from most kids' brains.

Not all people with autism are exactly alike, just like not all kids or teenagers are exactly alike. Many people with autism share some characteristics, though.

1. We have at least some difficulty with communication.

2. It's hard for us to understand social situations.

3. We tend to get really interested in one thing, which makes it hard to think about other things.

My goal is to help you better understand autism and the people who have it.

When I was 9 years old, I learned that I'm autistic. When I first heard that, I thought it meant that I'm a good artist (artistic!), which I am. But what it really means is I have autism. In my book, I use the word autistic to describe myself and others who have autism. Some people don't like the label "autistic," but in this book it's the easiest way to talk about people with autism, and I'm okay with it. I am autistic— but that's not all I am. I'm also:

Handy   Funny   Helpful   Generous

Creative   Curious   A talented golfer

Good at building and fixing things

You know what? Even though my brain is different, I'm still a kid. I like to have fun and want to have friends. My two best friends, Megan and Zak, are autistic, too. They invite me to do things, and we have lots of fun together. None of the other kids at my school invite me to birthday parties or to hang out. Some of them talk to me, and some don't. I'm lonely lots of the time, and I think other autistic kids are lonely, too.

It can take more time and patience to be friends with autistic kids, but it might be worth it because we will probably teach you something new. When I'm interested in a subject, I learn everything I can about it. For the past few months, I've been fascinated by everything Australian. Mate, I can teach you about kangaroos, joeys (baby kangaroos), koala bears, and other Australian animals. I could also teach you about some of the fun words Australians say, like "blimey" and "crikey." These words make me laugh.

How to Talk to an Autistic Kid is about more than just talking. I wrote it to help people get along better with autistic kids. You'll find ideas about hanging out and doing things with autistic kids and being a good friend, too. I want to help kids *without* autism feel comfortable around kids *with* autism. I hope fewer autistic kids will feel lonely.

If we are friendly and nice to each other, all of us can have new, interesting, and fun friends.

Daniel Stefanski

Say hi

I want to be included just like anyone else. I may be different, but I'm a person, too.

People are different in many ways: skin color, eye color, hairstyle, background, beliefs, you name it!

It feels good when people say hi to me, wave, and notice I'm here. Please don't ignore autistic kids just because they're different.

Talk to me

Everyone has different ways of talking. Some people talk a lot, some are quieter. Some people ask a lot of questions, and others like to tell stories and jokes. Well, just like anyone else, people with autism have different ways of talking. Some of us say a lot, some a little bit, and some nothing at all. Communicating is hard for us.

For me, my words get jumbled up when I talk. Sometimes I make goofy noises when I don't know what to say. Sometimes I repeat myself.

I know my way of communicating is different, but I like it when others listen. Then I feel included. Try to be patient when talking with an autistic kid.

What I "hear"

A lot of kids with autism are really smart, even if they have language difficulties. We can hear and talk and listen, like you. Sometimes you may have to slow down when you talk to us or reword what you say. No big deal. If people ask me, "Daniel, did you get what I just said?" it clues me in that I missed something. You might want to try that with other autistic kids.

Many autistic kids aren't good at understanding figures of speech. We think words mean *exactly* what they say. If you say, "Go jump in a lake," we might think you really mean for us to do it. My brother told me to "bug off," and then laughed at me when I tried to swipe a bug off of him.

What I don't "see"

Do you know what "body language" is? That's what your body says without words. When you shrug or raise your eyebrows, that means something. How you stand, what you do with your hands, and all your facial expressions mean something, too. You probably "read" people's body language without really thinking about it, but autistic kids often miss it—or misunderstand it. We also have trouble "getting" sarcasm and slang, two things middle school kids use a lot!

So if you say, "Nice shirt" while rolling your eyes, I probably won't get it that you're making a sarcastic joke.

My mom calls things like body language and sarcasm "social cues." Because I don't understand these cues (I call them "clues"), it's difficult to make friends and get along with other people.

embarrassed

angry

Lots of autistic kids have trouble looking other people in the eye. I'm not trying to be rude if I don't look at your face when I'm talking with you.

I'm not sure why,
        but it's easier for me to look down.

Please don't get frustrated,
raise your voice,
or shout.

When I get stuck

Sometimes thoughts get stuck in my head, and I go on and on about a subject that "wows" me, like Australia. I don't mean to be pushy, and I don't want to bore you! It relaxes me to talk about my favorite subject, but sometimes it's like my brain gets stuck and I need to be snapped out of it. I can get stuck on things I'm doing, too. Like I might not want to quit playing a video game, even if other kids are waiting to play.

14

You could say:

"Okay, I get what you're saying, but can we talk about something else now?"

"Can we try something different for a while? How about ..."

"I'm tired of this game. Let's do a different one."

You can also show me things you are interested in, like one of your books or games.

Let's hang out

I love to play golf. I also love Star Wars. Like anybody else, I also like doing things with friends— people like you!

To get to know me better, you could invite me to ride bikes, play video games, or go swimming. (Some autistic kids can do these things, and some aren't able to. Check with the person's mom or dad first.) I'm not good at team sports, but I can play individual sports like golf, bowling, tag, or ping-pong with you. We can play video games or board games like chess, or we can make stuff together.

Different is okay

How do you spot someone who's autistic? Sometimes you can't. We usually look just like anyone else, but if you spend time with us, you might notice big or little differences in how we act.

I saw an autistic kid flap his arms like a wattlebird.

Some autistic kids might rock back and forth or side-to-side.

They might do these things when they are nervous or upset about something. Or it might be a habit. They might not realize they're doing it.

Sometimes I hum loudly or buzz like a bee to calm down. It's part of my autism. Maybe you know someone who has an unusual habit, or maybe you have one of your own! Whether we have autism or not, everyone does things sometimes that make others go "Huh?"

BZZZZ

We're all human.

My mom read somewhere that Albert Einstein might have had Asperger's disorder, a mild kind of autism. She sometimes calls me "little Einstein." Like me, Einstein liked to wear the same style clothes again and again. He had lots of pairs of the same shirts and pants. I do, too.

Many autistic kids are sensitive to the feel of clothes. Certain clothes make our skin hurt or itch or both. That's why when we find a style of clothes we like, we stick with it.

In fact, all five senses can bother autistic kids very much. The five senses are:

sight

sound

smell

taste

touch

Not every autistic kid is the same, though. Perfumes and other smells can be very distracting to some kids. Fluorescent lights can hurt others. And for some, even soft touches can feel like pain. Loud noises and hard fabrics bother me most. Zak is bothered most by taste, especially foods with thick textures (but he loves hamburgers with ketchup).

Has anyone ever told you to use your "inside voice"? That's something autistic kids need to be reminded of sometimes. We might talk too loud for the situation, or other times we might drone on in a flat, boring voice. When these things happen, you can say . . .

"I'm interested in what you're saying, but could you keep your voice down?"

"That sounds pretty cool, Daniel, but would you mind if we change the subject?"

Some autistic kids might stand too close when they talk to you. We don't realize we're invading your space. You can just say . . .

"Excuse me, could you step back just a bit? I need a little more space."

27

Some people with autism have seizures, like my friend Megan. If your autistic friend has a medical condition in addition to having autism, you might have questions about that. Ask your friend if he or she is okay talking about it.

Zak doesn't have seizures, but he wears a hearing aide. He hears me when we talk about Star Wars. He doesn't hear so well when his mom asks for help around the house.

Be a good friend

Don't feel sorry for me. I have autism, but I'm cool with who I am. I love lots of things about my life: my family, my pets, my friends, and learning about things like astronomy, engineering, plants, animals, the weather, and how things work. I feel good when I take care of sick and homeless animals at the shelter where I volunteer. Another thing I enjoy is helping teach others about autism.

It's easy to be a good friend to an autistic kid. Ask about my life. Ask me what I like to do. Laugh *with* me and not *at* me. (I can tell the difference, even if it seems like I can't.)

Being a good friend means showing me respect. Sometimes, kids who are stronger or smarter might want to show off by hurting or teasing an autistic kid. Once, some kids from my school were at the driving range at the same time I was. They called me names and laughed at me, and I could tell they thought I would fail.

I felt terrible!

But once they saw my swing, things changed. They were really impressed! They complimented me and asked me questions about golf. It felt good to be part of the group, at least for one day.

Just because autistic kids seem different doesn't mean it's okay to tease or bully them. Everyone is different in some way.

If you see an autistic kid—or any kid—being bullied or teased, you can help that person by sticking up for him or her. Tell a teacher or another adult if someone is being threatened or hurt. You will feel good about yourself. You will be a hero.

If you hurt an autistic kid's feelings, you can make things better by apologizing. Autistic kids have feelings, just like you.

Reach out

Sometimes you might see autistic kids alone
at recess, in the cafeteria, or somewhere else.
If you do, they are probably lonely.
Ask them to do something,
or invite them to
hang out. Compliment
them when they do
something interesting
or cool.

You can volunteer to be a school buddy to an autistic student, or ask a teacher, counselor, or principal to help you form a buddy program if there isn't one.

In buddy programs, you learn about different kinds of disabilities and spend time with special needs kids at your school. You might do schoolwork or eat lunch together, join a school club, or just hang out. You help autistic (and other special needs) kids learn social skills and feel accepted.

Another way you can help is by explaining what you know about autism to other kids. The more people understand, the better we'll all get along.

Brothers and sisters of autistic kids need friends and support, too—just like anyone. My brother sometimes feels protective of me, and sometimes he's embarrassed. I understand that, even though it makes me sad or mad sometimes.

You can help siblings of autistic kids just by hanging out with them and letting them talk about their feelings. Let them know it's not bad or uncommon to feel embarrassed, lonely, frustrated, or upset.

There are good things about having an autistic brother or sister. The sibling will probably grow up to be patient, caring, tolerant, and independent. That's pretty great!

How do you talk to an autistic kid?

Respectfully

Kindly

Compassionately

Eagerly

Thoughtfully

Helpfully

Patiently

With friendship, acceptance, honesty, caring, and humor.

Having autism makes me a little different from other kids, but in the most important ways, we're all pretty similar. I have goals and dreams, just like you do.

I want to go to college and learn more about computer animation. I want to invent computer games for kids with disabilities. I want to beat my stepdad at golf, grow taller than my brother, and build my mom a big, beautiful tree house so she can have a place to relax and read. I want to get married. I want to write another book. And I want to travel and share this book with people all over the world.

I will always have autism, but that doesn't mean my future won't be great.

About the author

Daniel Stefanski is 14 years old and a middle school student. He has a passion for writing and drawing and likes to declare proudly "I'm autistic and artistic."

A talented golfer, Daniel has participated in the Special Olympics and other competitive golf events. At age 4, he was adopted from an orphanage in Bulgaria and flew eighteen hours with his new mom to his new home in Valparaiso, Indiana. An animal lover and shelter volunteer, Daniel is surrounded by the love of his mom, dad, stepfather, brother, and five dogs.

Other Great Books from Free Spirit

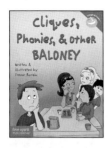

Cliques, Phonies, & Other Baloney
by Trevor Romain
If you're on the outside, you're treated like dirt. If you're on the inside, you have to follow the rules. Who needs more rules? This book helps kids deal with cliques and learn how to make real friends. For ages 8–13.
136 pp.; softcover; illust.; 5¹/₈" x 7"

Your Life in Comics
100 Things for Guys to Write and Draw
by Bill Zimmerman, artwork by Tyler Page
Rather than provide the story, this interactive book for guys allows them to decide what happens by using words and drawings of their creation. Some of the activities include completed comics where boys can dictate what happens through dialogue. Others encourage them to draw comic strips. Freestyle activities let guys personalize the book in fun ways. For ages 9–13.
128 pp.; softcover; 2-color illust.; 6" x 9"

Good-Bye Bully Machine
by Debbie Fox and Allan L. Beane, Ph.D., illustrated by Debbie Fox
Kids learn what bullying is, why it hurts, and what they can do to end it with this fresh, compelling book. With its sophisticated collage art, lively layout, and straightforward text, *Good-Bye Bully Machine* engages kids and keeps them engaged. Adults who share this book with kids can raise awareness and increase empathy by talking about bullying behaviors as fuel for the machine—and kind behaviors as ways to dismantle it. For ages 8 & up.
48 pp.; hardcover; color illust.; 8¼" x 8¼"
48 pp.; softcover; color illust.; 8" x 8"

Interested in purchasing multiple quantities? Contact edsales@freespirit.com or call 1.800.735.7323 and ask for Education Sales.

Many Free Spirit authors are available for speaking engagements, workshops, and keynotes. Contact speakers@freespirit.com or call 1.800.735.7323.

For pricing information, to place an order, or to request a free catalog, contact:

Free Spirit Publishing Inc.
217 Fifth Avenue North • Suite 200 • Minneapolis, MN 55401-1299
toll-free 800.735.7323 • local 612.338.2068
fax 612.337.5050 • help4kids@freespirit.com• www.freespirit.com